QUICK GUIDE TO FINANCIAL SKILLS

# QUICK GUIDE TO JOBS AND TAXES

by Marne Ventura

BrightPoint Press

San Diego, CA

an imprint of ReferencePoint Press, Inc.
Printed in the United States

For more information, contact:
BrightPoint Press
PO Box 27779
San Diego, CA 92198
www.BrightPointPress.com



LIBRARY OF CONGRESS CATALOGING-IN-PUBLICATION DATA

Name: Ventura, Marne, author.
Title: Quick Guide to Jobs and Taxes / by Marne Ventura.
Description: San Diego, CA: BrightPoint Press, Inc., 2025 | Series: Quick Guide to Financial Skills | Includes bibliographical references and index. | Audience: Grades 7 to 9
Identifiers: ISBN: 9781678209063 (hardcover) | ISBN: 9781678209070 (eBook)
The complete Library of Congress record is available at www.loc.gov.

# CONTENTS

# AT A GLANCE

- People earn money to pay for needs, wants, and savings. To earn money, people do jobs providing goods or services that other people need or want.

- Young teens can earn money by doing jobs such as babysitting or pet care. Older teens can work for businesses. Employers must follow child labor laws.

- Employers must pay workers at least the federal minimum wage. Some states have their own requirements for a higher minimum wage.

- Job-posting websites are useful for finding jobs. A résumé and cover letter are important tools for job applicants.

- Federal, state, and city governments collect taxes from people. Income tax, property tax, and sales tax are three types of tax that people pay.

- Tax money is used to run the government. It pays for services that benefit taxpayers.

- The Internal Revenue Service (IRS) collects income tax. Taxpayers file an income tax return each year. People who have paid too much income tax during the year get a tax refund after they file their tax return. People who have not paid enough will owe the government money.

- Adjusted gross income is a person's total income minus their deductions. Taxpayers owe a percentage of their adjusted gross income to state and federal governments.

# TARA'S FIRST PAYCHECK

Tara went into the sandwich shop on her way home from school. Today was payday. Tara was excited to get her very first paycheck. Before she turned 16, she worked in her neighborhood. She babysat the Wilson children next door. She walked and fed Riley and Casey's dog when they were out of town. For those jobs, she got paid with cash on the same day she did the job.

**Many teens work in food service or retail.**

Her new job was different. She worked 10 hours per week. Her **wage** was $15.50 per hour. Tara's paycheck today was for her first two weeks of work. She was looking forward to putting $310 into her bank account.

Tara's manager was behind the counter. He smiled and handed Tara an envelope. "Congratulations, Tara! Here's your first paycheck."

Tara thanked him and hurried outside. She ripped open the envelope. To her surprise, the check was for $255.28. The pay stub attached to the check listed $310 as Tara's gross earnings. But listed underneath were **FICA** Social Security, FICA Medicare, and **Federal**

## TARA'S PAY STUB

**Company Details**
The Best Sandwich Shop
824 Bologna Ave
Sacramento, CA 95814

| Employee | Employee ID | Pay Period |
|---|---|---|
| Tara Lim | 2859027 | 10/22/24–11/04/24 |

| | Period Hours | Period Earnings |
|---|---|---|
| Regular | 20 | 310.00 |
| Overtime | 0 | 0.00 |
| **Total** | 20 | 310.00 |
| Base rate | | 15.50 |

| Deductions | Period |
|---|---|
| FICA Social Security | 19.22 |
| FICA Medicare | 4.50 |
| Fed Tax Withholding | 31.00 |
| **Total deductions** | 54.72 |
| Gross pay | 310.00 |
| Net pay | 255.28 |

**The pay stub attached to Tara's first paycheck shows her earnings and deductions for her first two weeks of work. This is an estimated example. Every person's tax situation is different. State and local taxes vary.**

Tax Withholding. Each listing had an amount subtracted from the $310.

Tara called her older brother Robbie. He used to work at the same shop before going to college.

"Hey Tara!" Robbie answered. "What's up?"

"I just got my first paycheck," she said. "But it seems like they didn't pay me enough! They subtracted a bunch of money."

"Those are taxes," Robbie said. "Didn't you have to fill out a W-4 tax form when you started?"

**US workers fill out a W-4 form to determine how much tax will be withheld from their paychecks.**

Tara vaguely remembered a form about taxes. But she hadn't really understood it. Her mom had helped her fill it out. "So, I'm not really getting $15.50 per hour? What is all this stuff, anyway?" Tara asked.

"The government requires you to pay into Social Security and Medicare," Robbie said. "People pay into these programs throughout their working lives. Then they can use them when they're older. When you reach **retirement** age, you'll get a monthly Social Security check. It gives you income when you're no longer working. Medicare is health insurance. It helps pay for doctors and medicine when you are over a certain age."

"And then there's *more* tax on top of that?" Tara asked.

**People have to pay sales tax for some purchases, but rules vary. Some stores in airports or tourist areas do not have to charge tax.**

"Yes. The withheld tax goes to the federal government. The government uses tax money to pay for things like roads and schools. Next year you'll file a tax return.

If you've earned enough to pay taxes, the government will keep the amount subtracted from your checks. Some people pay too much throughout the year. They get a tax refund. Since you're only working part time, you might get all your taxes refunded."

"That could be good," Tara said. She was still disappointed about her paycheck. But she was glad she understood more about it.

## JOBS AND TAXES

Founding father Benjamin Franklin said, "In this world, nothing is certain except death and taxes."[1] Taxes may be charged on what a person earns, buys, or owns. The most common way to earn income is through a job. Learning how to apply for jobs helps people find the right job for them.

# CHAPTER ONE

# EARNING MONEY

Everyone requires money for wants and needs. Needs are **vital** things, such as food and shelter. Wants are things that are nice to have, such as video games or music lessons. A third reason to earn money is to save. People save money to pay for emergencies. They save for college or weddings. They save for retirement. People earn money by providing goods or services that other people want or need.

**Earning an income allows people to save money for important expenses.**

Eve Tahmincioglu writes about business and finance. She says, "Sometimes a job is not your dream job but is all about paying

**Many young people's first introduction to work is doing odd jobs for cash, such as walking dogs or housesitting.**

the bills. There's nothing wrong with that, and lots of people do this."[2] But many people work for reasons other than just earning money. Some work to help others. Some work to earn respect. Some just really enjoy doing a certain kind of work. Steve Jobs was the cofounder of Apple. He said, "Your work is going to fill a large part of your life, and the only way to be truly satisfied is to do what you believe is great work. And the only way to do great work is to love what you do."[3]

## FINDING A JOB

Young people often find jobs in their neighborhoods. Common first jobs are yard work, babysitting, or pet care. Older students might be hired to work in community businesses. Some young people start their own businesses.

When Jarod turned 16, he wanted a part-time job. His older brother showed him how to use a job posting website. Jarod set a filter. He searched for jobs that didn't require a degree. One job was at a local sporting goods store. Jarod didn't know much about sports. His hobbies were drawing, painting, and pottery. Another job came up at a nearby art supply store. That was a much better fit! He decided to apply.

Jarod filled out a form online. He entered contact information. He gave his year in school. He listed what hours he could work. The form asked for three references. The store's manager would call these people. She would ask them if they thought Jarod

Many students ask trusted teachers to act as job references.

would make a good employee. Jarod checked with his art teacher, a neighbor whose children he babysat, and another neighbor whose dog he walked. They all said he could use them as references.

## LAWS AND RULES FOR YOUNG WORKERS

When a business hires a worker, there are certain laws it must follow. Federal law bans businesses from hiring workers younger than 14. These laws also limit the hours and types of work children under 16 can do. Children younger than 18 cannot be hired for dangerous work. Rules for children working on farms vary by state.

Children under 14 can babysit, deliver newspapers, work as actors, or do yardwork. They can work in their family's business if the work isn't dangerous. Children who are 14 or 15 can work up to 3 hours on school days. They can work up to 8 hours on non-school days. Children who are 16 or 17 can work full time if the job is not dangerous. Once people turn 18, there are no federal limits on what kinds of jobs they can work.

## Work Permits

Each state has its own child labor laws. For example, **minors** in California must get a work permit. Work permits are usually given out at school. The minor's parent or guardian must sign the permit. So must the employer. Students must attend school regularly if they want to work. If a job is harming a student's education, the school can **revoke** the work permit.

**The youth minimum wage allows companies to pay a lower minimum wage to workers under 20 for the first 90 days of their employment.**

**Employers** must pay all workers at least the federal minimum wage. In 2024, this was $7.25 per hour. Some states and cities have a higher minimum wage. In some jobs, workers earn tips. These jobs may be allowed to pay a lower minimum wage.

A first job may not be what someone does forever. But first jobs are a good way to get started in the workforce. New employees learn to work with other people. They learn to show up on time. They learn to be organized and follow directions. They figure out what kind of work they want to do in the future.

# CHAPTER TWO

# APPLYING FOR A JOB

People who are looking for work can find jobs in different ways. Most people look for jobs online. Employers post job descriptions on websites. Applicants can find and sort information about suitable jobs in one place. Some people look for jobs in person. Stores or restaurants might display a "Now Hiring" sign. A job seeker can walk in and apply to these places. People can also find jobs through personal

**Businesses open to the public usually welcome walk-in applicants. This is especially true if they have "Now Hiring" or "Help Wanted" signs displayed. Stopping by in person is less accepted for private businesses.**

NOW
HIRING
Noodles.com/Careers
NOODLES
& COMPANY

connections. Job seekers might talk to family and friends. These people might have information about job opportunities.

When a person applies for a job, she needs to show the employer why she is qualified for the job. She must introduce

## Avoiding Gimmicks

Job applicants want to stand out. Candidates sometimes send gifts to managers. One sent a shoe to "get a foot in the door." But workplace advice writer Alison Green says these gimmicks can hurt a person's chances. "The reality is that the way to stand out . . . is pretty boring," Green says. "Be highly qualified for the job, have a strong résumé showing a track record of achievement, and write a compelling cover letter that explains why you'd excel at the role."

*Alison Green, "The Guy Who Sent a Hiring Manager a Box with a Shoe in It to 'Get a Foot in the Door,'"* Slate, *February 4, 2019. http://slate.com.*

herself to the employer. She does this using a résumé and a cover letter. A résumé is a list of a person's job experience, training, and skills. A cover letter introduces an applicant. It explains why she is interested in the job and would be good at it.

## WRITING A RÉSUMÉ

Maria just graduated from high school. She thinks she wants to become an elementary school teacher. She has decided to live at home for a year and work full time. This will help her save money for college. She wants to find a job in an elementary school. This will help her decide if teaching is the right career path.

Maria looks at a job-posting website. She finds openings for teachers' aides at several nearby schools. The website asks Maria to upload her résumé. Maria has never had a résumé before. She looks for advice on how to write one. She finds samples online.

Maria begins with her name and contact information. Many of the examples Maria found have a Profile or Highlights section next. This is optional. This section is a short summary about the applicant. It highlights some of the most important information. Alison Green runs the *Ask a Manager* advice website. She says, "Try thinking about what you'd want a contact to say if they had 20 seconds to sum you up to someone who was hiring for the work you do."[4]

The next part of the résumé is the most important. Maria lists her previous experience. She should list the business, her job title, and when she worked there. She lists her job duties. She should also mention any achievements. Maria hasn't ever had a formal job. But she can add her babysitting experience. She could also list leadership positions from her clubs. Next comes the Education section. Maria should

**The Profile or Highlights section may also be referred to as a Summary or Objective.**

list her school and graduation date. Her GPA was 3.8. She can include that, too.

There are more optional sections Maria can include. She could add a section on her skills. She could list her clubs and other activities. Some people share their hobbies. These sections are less common for people with more experience. But Maria is just starting out. These sections could give helpful information to the employer. Experienced workers can have two-page résumés. But Maria should stick to one page. She should also carefully check her résumé for spelling mistakes.

Green says there are few strict résumé rules. "You can give your résumé to 10 different people who know what they're doing, and you'll get 10 different sets of

Maria Alvarez

1922 Address St. Topeka, KS 66546 | (555) 555-0123 | name@email.com | Website or LinkedIn profile

Recent high school graduate seeking work in education and childcare. Responsible and motivated worker who exceeds expectations.

***Education***

**General Diploma** | Washington High School; Topeka, KS **May 2024**

- GPA: 3.8
- Clubs: National Honor Society, Girls Soccer Team (Team Captain), Orchestra, Student Council (Treasurer)
- Honors: Honor roll, service award honoree for hours volunteered at school

***Experience***

**Smith, Lopez, Peng Households** | Topeka, KS **Sept. 2020–Present**

Babysitter

- Supervised children ages five through twelve. Duties included playing games, cooking meals, and transporting them to activities.
- Researched, scheduled, and organized age-appropriate activities for daily summer care
- Adapted to last-minute care requests, demonstrating flexibility and skill in finding fun non-screen activities to keep children entertained
- Oversaw homework, providing tutoring help when needed
- Followed appointed sleep schedules, introducing various techniques to help children wind down in the evenings

***Skills and Certifications***

- CPR certified
- Spanish proficiency
- Licensed driver
- Organization
- Allergen-friendly meal preparation
- Conflict resolution
- Leadership
- Public speaking
- Teaching

***Volunteer Work***

- Tutoring program for children and peers
- Adopt-a-highway litter patrol

**When creating a résumé, people should use fonts that are easy to read.**

advice," she says.[5] It's most important that the résumé highlights a candidate's best qualities.

## COVER LETTER

Experts advise job applicants to write a one-page cover letter to go with a résumé. The cover letter lets applicants explain why they want a particular job. Applicants can also explain why they would be good at it. Cover letters do more than

**Job applicants should write a new cover letter each time they apply for a job.**

summarize a résumé. An applicant can add new information. She can share how her experience relates to the role. Jodi Glickman is a communications expert. She says, "[A cover letter is] your best chance of getting the attention of the human resources (HR) person or hiring manager and an important opportunity to distinguish yourself from everyone else."[6]

Résumés can be used to apply for multiple jobs. But applicants should write a new cover letter for each application. Cover letters should not be generic. Productivity expert Jill Duffy advises job applicants to read the job description carefully. They should look for keywords. Applicants can use those keywords when stating their experience and skills.

## THE NEXT STEPS

If an employer is impressed with the résumé and cover letter, the next step is an interview. Some employers start with phone or video interviews. These are often short. The interviewer asks basic questions. If a candidate seems like a good fit, she may be invited for an in-person interview.

Maria has an interview at one of the schools. She prepares ahead of time. Maria looks up common interview questions. She practices her answers out loud. She thinks of examples of her experience that fit the job description. She also does some research about the school.

On the day of the interview, Maria dresses professionally. Her clothes do not have wrinkles or holes. She arrives early to

**First impressions are important in an interview.**

her appointment. She is polite to the people she meets.

Some people print a paper copy of their résumé to bring to an interview. People applying for creative jobs might bring examples of their work. Others bring a small notebook and a pen to take notes. At the end of an interview, employers will usually

Some people send paper thank-you notes. These are preferred in some fields. But paper notes can take too long to arrive. They can get lost in the mail. Email is instant. Experts recommend email for most people.

ask if the applicant has any questions. Maria can ask questions if something was unclear. She can also ask about topics the interviewers didn't cover.

After returning home, Maria writes a thank-you note. These notes are usually sent by email. An applicant thanks the interviewers for their time. She should restate her interest in the position. She can talk about why she would be a good fit. She should bring up specific examples from the interview. This makes the note more personal. The next step is to wait for a job offer. If the offer is extended and the applicant accepts, she has a new job.

# CHAPTER THREE

# TAXES

US Supreme Court Justice Oliver Wendell Holmes said, "Taxes are what we pay for civilized society."[7] A civilized society has a government. The government works to protect its people. It passes laws to keep people safe. It uses tax money to fund services for the community. Taxes help pay for roads, schools, police and fire departments, and more.

**Taxes help pay for public services such as libraries.**

People who earn money pay income tax. When people spend money, they pay sales tax. People also pay tax on property they own. These taxes are collected by federal, state, and local governments.

## TYPES OF TAXES

The federal government charges income tax on people's earnings. Most states also charge income tax. Tax rates change based on the earner's income. The more money a person earns, the higher the tax rate.

The federal government also charges Social Security and Medicare tax. These are called FICA taxes. When people reach retirement age, they can collect Social Security checks. Social Security funds are also paid to children whose parents have died. People who are disabled and cannot work may receive Social Security as well. People of retirement age can receive Medicare health insurance. Employers deduct FICA taxes from their workers' paychecks. They send this money to the federal government.

State and local governments charge property tax. People who own land and buildings pay property tax. Some state and local governments also charge personal

**All states charge some kind of property tax. But some states waive or reduce property tax for people over 65.**

property tax. People who own cars, boats, or **investments** such as stocks or bonds might have to pay this tax.

Some state and local governments also charge sales tax. People pay this when they buy goods and services. Sales tax is charged as a percentage of the cost of something. For example, Ethan buys a car for $10,000. His state's sales tax rate is 7.25 percent. He would pay $725 in tax.

## Sales Tax and Groceries

Most states do not charge sales tax on groceries. Of states that do, most charge a lower tax rate than the general sales tax. Critics of grocery taxes say these taxes hurt lower-income people. Defenders say the money helps pay for public services such as education.

## HOW TAXES ARE USED

Governments use tax money to run the government. Tax money pays for the country's infrastructure. It also pays for public services and the military.

Infrastructure is the basic physical system of a business, region, or country. Roads, bridges, and transportation systems are examples. Both federal and state governments use tax money to pay for infrastructure.

Public services include schools, parks, and police and fire departments. Public schools and local parks are mostly paid for with property taxes. These are usually collected by local governments. Local governments pay for most police departments. Fire departments are

**Congress uses some taxpayer money to pay for national parks.**

also usually funded by state and local governments. States that charge sales tax use it for different things. It might be used for any of the services offered by the state.

The federal government spends about 20 percent of its tax money on defense and security. This includes the cost of the military. It also includes the Department of Homeland Security. The Transportation Security Administration (TSA) is in charge of airport security. Its budget is also included.

Some people complain about paying taxes. Diane Lim Rogers is an American economist. She points out the benefits of taxes. Rogers writes,

> *The revenues provided by taxes strengthen, not weaken, our nation's economy. They fund essential public goods and services, they contribute positively to national saving, and many of the things that they fund—from highways to schools to biomedical research and national parks—indirectly create private wealth as well.*[8]

# TAX RETURNS

People who earn money report their earnings to the Internal Revenue Service (IRS). This is the federal agency that collects taxes. The IRS provides forms to help people report their income. These forms are due each year on April 15. When people submit these forms, they are filing a tax return.

The IRS calculates how much tax a person owes. It starts with the total amount

**Filing taxes involves a lot of paperwork.**

1040
U.S. Ind
For the year Jan. 1–Dec. 31, 2015, or othe
Your first name and initial
If a joint return, spouse's first name and in
Home address (number and street). If you have
City, town or post office, state, and ZIP code. If you hav
Foreign country name
Filing Status
Check only one box.
Single
Married
Exemptions
Yourself.
Spouse
Dependents:
(1) First name
Income
Attach Form(s) W-2 here. Also attach Forms W-2G and
Total number
Wages, salari
Taxable int
Adjusted Gross Income
Refund
Direct deposit? See instructions and fill in 48b, 48c, and 48d or Form 8888.
Credit for child and dep
Credit for the elderly
Schedule R.
Form 2441.
Add lines 28 and 29.
If you did not get a W-2, see instructions.
Privacy Act, an

**People who earned less than a certain amount may not need to file an income tax return. In 2023, a single person under the age of 65 who earned less than $13,850 did not have to pay income taxes.**

of income a person has earned during the year. It allows taxpayers to deduct, or subtract, certain expenses from their income. These are called deductions. The result is the taxpayer's adjusted gross income. This amount is multiplied by a certain percentage to find the amount due. The percentage is determined by a person's tax bracket. Different income levels are in different brackets.

## FILING A TAX RETURN

Employers give workers forms for their tax returns. Part-time and full-time workers get W-2 forms. A W-2 shows a person's total income for the year. It also shows how much the employer withheld for federal and state income tax. People might need other

**Some people hire a professional to help with their taxes. Others use tax software or file on their own.**

tax forms, too. There are forms for income earned through investments. People might need forms related to health insurance, childcare, or student loan costs. Taxpayers also need receipts for expenses that might be deductions. Charitable donations are one example. Large purchases such as a vehicle or a home are another.

Taxpayers can file their returns online or by mail. To file by mail, taxpayers can go to www.IRS.gov. They can download and print the forms they need. They can fill them out by hand and mail them. Taxpayers can also file online. People can file online for free through the IRS. Taxpayers can also buy software that helps them file online. These programs often offer help from professionals. In addition, taxpayers can pay an accountant to prepare their tax return.

## DEDUCTIONS

Credits and deductions can lower a person's tax bill. Credits are subtracted from the amount of tax due. Deductions are subtracted from a person's taxable income. Both help reduce the amount of tax a person pays. Some states offer a clean car credit. Someone who bought an electric or hybrid car might get a credit. People who install solar panels can also get tax credits.

Student loan interest or donations to charity count as deductions. The IRS has a standard deduction amount each year. In 2024, it was $14,600 for taxpayers filing individually. Taxpayers can use the standard deduction. Or they can list and add up their actual expenses. This is called an itemized deduction. Finance writer Ana Staples explains how to decide which deduction to use. She says, "Sum up itemized deductions and see if they'll turn out to

**Deductions and credits can add up to big tax breaks.**

be more than the standard deduction. If not, don't itemize, because the standard deduction will save you more money."[9]

Staples advises first-time filers to check for one more thing. "Talk to your parents to see if they're claiming you as a dependent," she says. "This can be the case if you still live with them or they offer substantial financial help. You'll still have to file your taxes, but your parents will get certain tax benefits."[10]

## CHECKING THE BALANCE

After a taxpayer files his return, the IRS checks how much he's paid. If the right amount of money was withheld, the process ends. Sometimes the taxpayer didn't pay enough. Then he'll owe more money. If he paid too much, he'll get a refund. If a taxpayer owes more than he can pay, he can ask the IRS to set up a payment plan. The taxpayer commits to paying a certain amount each month.

## Are Refunds Good?

Getting a tax refund can feel exciting. It's better than owing money. But experts warn that a big refund isn't always good. "If you got a tax refund, that means that the federal government overcharged you for your income taxes," says financial writer and podcaster Nicole Lapin. "The government basically took out a loan from *your* paycheck and then paid it back to you *without interest*." People who receive a large refund might want to adjust how much tax is withheld from their paychecks.

*Nicole Lapin, "You Do Not Want a Tax Refund. Here's Why,"* Forbes, *October 25, 2021. www.forbes.com.*

Understanding how jobs and taxes work is an important key to success.

There will be an additional fee added to the tax amount due. There is also a fee for taxpayers who miss the April 15 deadline.

## FIRST STEPS

Finding a job and filing a tax return are major steps in becoming an adult. Earning and spending money are important actions for members of society. Knowing how to build a résumé, get work experience, and find a meaningful career are important life skills. When people pay taxes, they are contributing to the systems and services that benefit themselves and others.

# GLOSSARY

**employers**

people who hire and pay other people to do a job

**federal**

having to do with the central government of a country

**FICA**

short for Federal Insurance Contributions Act, taxes employers must withhold to fund Social Security and Medicare

**investments**

something purchased, such as real estate or gold, with the goal of earning more money than it cost

**minors**

young people who are not yet adults

**retirement**

the period of life where people have ended their career work

**revoke**

to take something away after it has been given

**vital**

very important, needed to maintain life

**wage**

a payment of money for work

# SOURCE NOTES

## INTRODUCTION: TARA'S FIRST PAYCHECK

1. Quoted in NCC Staff, "Benjamin Franklin's Last Great Quote and the Constitution," *National Constitution Center*, November 13, 2023. http://constitutioncenter.org.

## CHAPTER ONE: EARNING MONEY

2. Eve Tahmincioglu, "Sometimes a Job Is Just a Paycheck," *NBC News*, April 25, 2010. www.nbcnews.com.

3. Steve Jobs, "You've Got to Find What You Love," *Stanford News*, June 12, 2005. http://news.stanford.edu.

## CHAPTER TWO: APPLYING FOR A JOB

4. Alison Green, "My Step-by-Step Guide to Writing a Résumé," *Ask a Manager*, February 11, 2020. www.askamanager.org.

5. Alison Green, "Help! I'm Getting Confusing and Conflicting Résumé Advice!" *Ask a Manager*, September 20, 2012. www.askamanager.org.

6. Quoted in Amy Gallo, "How to Write a Cover Letter," *Harvard Business Review*, December 23, 2020. http://hbr.org.

7. Quoted in Eric A. San Juan, "Who Pays the Price of Civilization?" *Colombia Journal of Tax Law, 9*(1), 45–66. http://doi.org/10.7916/cjtl.v9i1.2858.

8. Diane Lim Rogers, "Good Reasons for Taxes," *Brookings*, April 16, 2006. www.brookings.edu.

## CHAPTER FOUR: TAX RETURNS

9. Ana Staples, "How to File Taxes for the First Time," *Bankrate*, March 24, 2021. www.bankrate.com.

10. Staples, "How to File Taxes for the First Time."

# FOR FURTHER RESEARCH


## BOOKS

Jennifer Boothroyd, *Taxes*. Minneapolis, MN: Bearport, 2023.

DK, *Careers*: *The Ultimate Guide to Planning Your Future*. New York: DK Publishing, 2022.

Emma Huddleston, *Finding a Job*. San Diego, CA: BrightPoint Press, 2020.

## INTERNET SOURCES

"Do Teens Have to File Taxes? A Beginner's Guide," *TaxSlayer*, March 25, 2024. www.taxslayer.com/blog.

"How To Find a Job as a Teenager (Plus Benefits and Job Types)," *Indeed Career Guide*, January 30, 2023. www.indeed.com/career-advice.

"What Teens Need to Know about Taxes," *Get Schooled*, February 29, 2024. http://getschooled.com.

## WEBSITES

### CareerOneStop
**www.careeronestop.org**

Sponsored by the US Department of Labor, this site offers various resources to job seekers, including career guidance and job search tools.

### How Money Smart Are You?
**http://playmoneysmart.fdic.gov**

The FDIC is a government agency that oversees financial institutions. This suite of resources includes fourteen games to help educate people on various financial skills.

### IRS
**www.irs.gov**

The IRS website includes tax withholding calculators, informational articles about taxes, resources for filing tax returns, and more.

# INDEX

# IMAGE CREDITS

Cover: © Halfpoint/Shutterstock Images
5: © Nomad_Soul/Shutterstock Images
7: © Anon_Tae/Shutterstock Images
9: © Red Line Editorial
10: © Piotr Swat/Shutterstock Images
12: © Roberto La Rosa/Shutterstock Images
15: © Dejan Dundjerski/Shutterstock Images
16: © hedgehog94/Shutterstock Images
19: © VH-Studio/Shutterstock Images
22: © Bignai/Shutterstock Images
25: © Andriy Blokhin/Shutterstock Images
29: © Anatoly Vartanov/Shutterstock Images
31: © Red Line Editorial
32: © EkaterinaN/Shutterstock Images
35: © Queenmoonlite Studio/Shutterstock Images
36: © Avava/Shutterstock Images
39: © Zoran Zeremski/Shutterstock Images
41: © Artazum/Shutterstock Images
44: © Wangkun Jia/Shutterstock Images
47: © RomanR/Shutterstock Images
48: © Prostock-Studio/Shutterstock Images
50: © Zivica Kerkez/Shutterstock Images
53: © fizkes/Shutterstock Images
56: © Okrasiuk/Shutterstock Images

# ABOUT THE AUTHOR

Marne Ventura is the author of more than one hundred books for young people. A former elementary teacher, she holds a Master's Degree in Reading and Language Development from the University of California. Ventura's nonfiction titles cover a wide range of topics, including finance, careers, STEM, arts and crafts, food and cooking, biographies, health, and survival. Ventura and her family live in California.